D0481535

SAGITTARIUS

This Book Belongs To

———————————————

SAGITTARIUS

The Sign of the Archer
November 23–December 21

By Teresa Celsi
and Michael Yawney

Ariel Books

Andrews and McMeel
Kansas City

SAGITTARIUS

ISBN: 0–8362–3077–9
Library of Congress Catalog Card Number: 93-73372

Contents

Astrology

An Introduction

Early in our history, as humankind changed from hunter-gatherers to farmers, they left the forests and moved to the plains, where they could raise plants and livestock. While they guarded their animals at night, the herders gazed up at the sky. They watched the stars circle Earth, counted the days between moons, and perceived an order in the universe.

Astrology was born as a way of finding a meaningful relationship between the movements of the heavens and the events on Earth. Astrologers believe that the celestial dance of planets affects our personalities and destinies. In order to better understand these forces, an astrologer creates a chart, which is like a snapshot of the heavens at the time of your birth. Each planet—Mercury, Venus, Mars, Jupiter, Saturn, Uranus, Neptune, and Pluto—has influence on you. So does the place of your birth.

The most important element in a chart is your sun sign, commonly known as your astrological sign. There are twelve signs of the zodiac, a belt of sky encircling Earth that is divided into twelve zones. Whichever zone the sun was in at your time of birth determines your sun sign. Your sun sign influences conscious behavior. Your moon sign influences unconscious behavior. (This book deals only with sun signs. To find your moon sign, you must look in a reference book or consult an astrologer.)

Each sign is categorized under one of the four elements: *fire, earth, air,* or *water.* Fire signs (Aries, Leo, and Sagittarius) are creative and somewhat self-centered. Earth signs (Taurus, Virgo, and Capricorn) are steady and desire material things. Air signs (Gemini, Libra, and Aquarius) are clever and intellectual.

Water signs (Cancer, Scorpio, and Pisces) are emotional and empathetic.

Each sign has one of three qualities—*cardinal*, *fixed*, or *mutable*—which shows how it operates. Cardinal signs (Aries, Cancer, Libra, and Capricorn) use their energy to lead in a direct, forceful way. Fixed signs (Taurus, Leo, Scorpio, and Aquarius) harness energy and use it to organize and consolidate. Mutable signs (Gemini, Virgo, Sagittarius, and Pisces) use energy to transform and change.

Every sign has a different combination of an element and a quality. When the positions of all the twelve planets are added to a chart, you can begin to appreciate the complexity of each individual. Astrology does not simplify people by shoving them into twelve personality boxes; rather, the details of your chart will be amazingly complex, inspiring the same awe those early herders must have felt while gazing up into the mystery of the heavens.

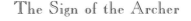

The Sign of the Archer

The sign of exploration and expansion, Sagittarius is always aiming for a distant target, like its symbol, the Archer.

This sign's ruling planet, Jupiter, can help explain Sagittarius's restless spirit. Jupiter, king of the gods in Roman mythology, was too powerful to be held back by anyone or anything. Whenever he felt restricted, he would change himself into an animal or bird and take off in search of new loves and new adventures. The Archer avoids restraints in a similar way—by questing for answers to life's many questions.

The Sagittarius symbol, a centaur aiming his bow and arrow, is a mythic combination of man and horse. Known for his wild adventures and vast knowledge, he was respected by princes and kings whose kingdoms prospered from the wisdom he shared with them. Like the centaur, the unselfish Sagittarius wants its knowledge (or money or power) to benefit the human community. If it doesn't, it loses all value to the Archer.

Character and Personality

S agittarius says "Yes!" to life. The Archer believes that good conquers evil, honesty is the best policy, and life is a banquet.

This attitude comes easily to those born under this sign because life is good to them. Or is life good to them because of this attitude? Either way, Sagittarius's supreme self-confidence allows it to believe it can handle anything. When adversity strikes, this sign works fearlessly to make things better—no matter how hopeless the situation may appear to an outsider.

A fire sign, Sagittarius is a bold and enthusiastic investigator with a wide range of interests. This sign wants to be in the know about everything—whether it's the latest trends in music, the most recent developments in science and technology, the trendiest new restaurants, or the hottest new vacation spots. However, Sagittarius is also a mutable (changeable) sign, so what interests the Archer one day may not interest it the next. The Archer can't abide being left behind and is continually seeking new targets.

Sagittarius is a theatrical creature who

hates to play the same role twice. The Archer hates to do *anything* twice. If you think you know a Sagittarius well, you may be in for a few surprises.

To the restless Archer, the chase is always more exciting than the capture—money and recognition from a job well done mean less than doing the job well. Sagittarius is easily bored and won't sit around resting on its laurels.

Restrictions annoy the Archer and commands and ultimatums will never work with this sign. Ask a Sagittarius for a favor and you've got it; tell a Sagittarius to do something and you've got trouble. The Archer is naturally giving and naturally rebellious.

And like other fire signs, Sagittarius has a temper. It doesn't arise often but when it does, watch out. The Archer never bears a grudge, however, and any flare-up will be over and forgotten in minutes.

Confident, open, and fun-loving, Sagittarius makes friends easily. But the Archer can also lose friends easily when it neglects to temper its absolute honesty with sympathy and tactfulness.

Signs and Symbols

Each sign in the zodiac is ruled by a different planet. Sagittarius is ruled by Jupiter, named after the king of the Roman gods. This sign is symbolized by the centaur, a mythical creature who is half horse, half archer.

The ninth sign of the zodiac, Sagittarius combines the element of fire (creativity) with the mutable (changeable) quality. The Archer is restless, outgoing, enthusiastic, optimistic, and philosophical.

The day of the week associated with this sign is Thursday. Sagittarius rules the hips, thighs, and liver. Deer, and all other hunted animals, are in its domain. Purple is its color, turquoise is its gemstone, and tin is its metal.

Flowers associated with the Archer are begonias, dandelions, and carnations. Grapefruits, raisins, and root vegetables are the foods connected to this sign.

Health and Fitness

ital, energetic Sagittarius loves physical activity—especially if it includes other people.

To keep fit, the Archer prefers team sports to solitary exercises like running or swimming. Aerobics classes will suit the Archer if the routines are challenging and the others in the class are friendly. (It was a Sagittarian, Jane Fonda, who made aerobics a household word.) Without the social component, Sagittarius will become antsy and bored.

Sagittarians may be accident prone. They love speed and action, and often misjudge their own strength and physical abilities. Luckily, the Archer has amazing recuperative powers. Few injuries leave any lasting damage.

Sagittarius has a tendency to overextend itself. It sometimes takes concerned friends to pressure the Archer to slow down and to relax. However, when the lighthearted Archer takes fitness seriously, this can be one of the strongest and healthiest signs of the zodiac.

Home and Family

Sagittarius values friendship more than kinship. In fact, the highest compliment an Archer can pay its parents is to declare that they are more like friends. The Archer may be close to family members, but blood isn't thicker than water to this sign.

As a parent, easygoing Sagittarius tends to be indulgent and may find it difficult to discipline a wayward child.

The Archer's impulse is to forgive and forget, so discipline usually falls to the other parent.

Housework can seem pointless to Sagittarius. Why make a bed when you'll just have to make it again tomorrow? Single Archers can live comfortably in a messy house. They would rather be out where the action is than at home doing the wash or running the vacuum. However, when they know that their efforts are appreciated by the people they live with, Sagittarians can be tireless housekeepers. They will maintain the home as a favor, but never as an obligation.

Careers and Goals

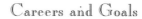

S agittarians are risk takers whose gambles frequently pay off. This optimistic sign often has business opportunites fall right into its lap.

Because they need variety, Archers do best at jobs with plenty of action, rather than repetitive, sedentary desk jobs. If they're challenged by their work, they are almost sure to excel.

Sagittarians seek work that gives

meaning to their lives and not just a regular paycheck. They like jobs that benefit others, especially children and animals. That's why many people born under this sign are drawn to the medical professions.

Archers make dynamic teachers who know how to make learning an adventure. Their enthusiasm for living and generosity of spirit inspire their students, no matter what subject they teach.

Fields that allow them to indulge their wanderlust and to be part of a team effort, like archaeology or anthropology, also appeal to the adventuresome Archer.

Pastimes and Play

Sagittarians always have some new hobby. Their interests continue to change throughout their lives.

Traveling always comes first. The more exotic the destination is, the better this sign will like it. Those Archers who can't get away enough will travel vicariously—reading travel books and watching films and documentaries shot in some exotic or offbeat locale.

True to the symbol for this sign, the Archer loves horses. In fact, Sagittarius is fascinated by anything with horse-power—including cars, boats, planes, and trains.

Sagittarians have a special love for animals. When they own pets, they enjoy doing things with them. Jogging with a dog or playing with a kitten is a pleasant way for the Archer to spend a few hours.

Volleyball, doubles tennis, multi-player board games—these are the games that appeal to the socially out-going Archer. It doesn't matter who wins or loses, as long as everyone has a good time.

Love Among the Signs

What is attraction? What is love? Throughout the centuries, science has tried and failed to come up with a satisfying explanation for the mysterious connection between two people.

For the astrologer, the answer is clear. The position of the planets at the time of your birth creates a pattern that influences you throughout your lifetime.

When your pattern meets another person's, the two of you might clash or harmonize.

Why this mysterious connection occurs can be explored only by completing charts for both individuals. But even if the chemistry is there, will it be a happy relationship? Will it last? No one can tell for certain.

Every relationship requires give-and-take, and an awareness of the sun sign relationships can help with this process. The sun sign influences conscious behavior. Does your lover catalog the items in the medicine cabinet? Chances are you have a Virgo on your hands. Do you like to spend your weekends running while

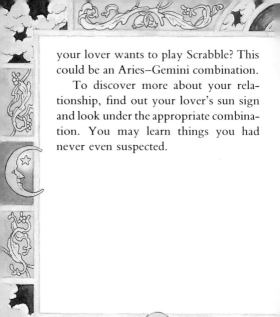

your lover wants to play Scrabble? This could be an Aries–Gemini combination.

To discover more about your relationship, find out your lover's sun sign and look under the appropriate combination. You may learn things you had never even suspected.

Sagittarius with Aries

(March 21–April 20)

One minute Sagittarius and Aries are locked in combat, spitting fire at each other. The next moment, they're locked in each other's arms, necking like teenagers.

The Archer and the Ram shoot straight from the hip and thrive on drama. Chances are, the first time they met they sized each other up on the spot, and made a date. These two signs waste no time on preliminaries and find the direct approach equally appealing in others.

These two will have no hidden agenda nor will they tolerate any festering resentments. If either one of them is angry, confrontation will be immediate—regardless of the time, place, or situation. When the confrontation is over, it will be forgotten and all will be forgiven.

Sagittarius and Aries are both wildly imaginative and know how to have fun together. Both love the outdoors and the excitement of team sports.

Because both are fire signs, they share a creative, optimistic outlook—though neither is very practical. Aries is focused, but has a tendency to set its goals so idealistically high that many become unobtainable; Sagittarius rarely focuses on goals—gambling its future on happenstance and good luck. If Lady Luck passes the Archer by, it may look to the Ram for support—at least until the next roll of the dice.

Fidelity will be a crucial issue with this pair. Though these passionate, impulsive fire signs can spark a hot romance, it could burn out quickly in jealous flames. The Archer craves variety and will have difficulty curbing its flirtatious nature in social situations. The Ram may occasionally stray, but under no circumstances will it forgive infidelity in a mate. It's unfair—but Aries isn't fair. The Archer must be willing to make some big adjustments in its social behavior.

Otherwise, this will be a smooth relationship since both are likely to agree on what is important in life. If the Aries drive becomes too much for the easygoing Archer, or if freewheeling Sagittarius seems too unmotivated to the Ram, it will be easy for these two to air their grievances and set themselves on a more positive course. Common interests and plenty of fun together can make this a long-run romance.

Sagittarius with Taurus

(April 21–May 21)

L et's get dressed up and go to that new restaurant," says Sagittarius. "I'd rather have a nice dinner at home and rent a video," answers Taurus.

Earthy, home-loving Taurus and fiery, gadabout Sagittarius view life in completely different ways. The Bull finds security in a comfortable nest, with a paid-up mortgage and two cars in the garage. To the Archer, home is a place to change clothes between trips or recharge its batteries for the next exciting adventure.

Taurus plays by the rules, working steadily and slowly, no matter how routine the job or mundane the task. Sagittarius can't abide rules and jumps right in, relying on luck and inspiration to see it through, which they often do.

Though Taurus is attracted to the Archer's zest for life, and Sagittarius finds the Bull's stability appealing, these same qualities might begin to grate on these two in time. Just when Sagittarius wants to strike out on some grand new adventure, the Bull may decide to plant its feet firmly in the earth. Compromise may be difficult here but it's essential for this relationship to succeed.

The Archer must also curb its roving eye—its friendly, flirty ways will make the Bull see red in no time. And unlike Sagittarius, Taurus doesn't readily forgive and forget.

These two could score big in business. The steady hard-working Bull could be a good partner for the creative, risk-taking Archer—provided, of course, that the risks aren't too great for the conservative Bull and the business isn't too confining for the footloose Archer.

In the bedroom, these two signs have different styles. Sagittarius wants excitement and fiery passion. Taurus wants slow, steady lovemaking—a style that appeals to many signs, but not to the Archer.

These signs have much to offer one another, however. Taurus can provide a stable base of operations as well as support for those times when the Archer's luck runs out. And Sagittarius's comic sense and sunny good humor could inspire the Bull to leave the corral once in a while for greener pastures. If both go into this relationship with their eyes open, they will learn a lot from each other—and have a good time doing it.

Sagittarius with Gemini

(May 22–June 21)

T here is a strong initial attraction between Gemini, the sign of the Twins, and Sagittarius. Both are restless, changeable, and loaded with charm.

In addition, each sees in the other qualities it wishes it had. The airy, intellectual Gemini likes the Archer's direct, personable style; Sagittarius appreciates the Twins' clear thinking, poise, and tactfulness—a good balance to the Archer's blunt honesty. The Archer's en-thusiasm is also a strong draw for the Twins—a cool, detached sign that can rarely muster the enthusiasm that comes so naturally to the vivacious Sagittarius.

Boredom is a constant threat to these two signs. Both enjoy life in the fast lane and absorb new experiences like sponges. They are sure to be a popular couple on the local social scene. Sagittarius's gift for comedy and Gemini's stylish wit often make these two the life of the party.

Commitment is hard for the Archer and the Twins. They may see each other more as playmates than friends. Gemini prefers casual relationships and Sagittarius likes to roam freely, so it may take these two quite some time to settle down. Bonding will most likely occur over a period of time if they have a common goal, a shared job, or any other strong mutual interest.

Though their similarities are numerous, there will be some rough waters for these two to navigate. For instance, their different approaches to the truth can throw them off course. Gemini is a born opportunist and often shades the truth for its own benefit. This might not sit too well with the compulsively honest Archer. If Sagittarius does exaggerate on occasion, it will be for the benefit of others, not for itself.

Sexually, these two are on the same wavelength. Life in the bedroom will be tender, playful, and lighthearted. Neither sign suffers from sexual jealousy—a big plus for these two since both love to flirt. And their full social calendars give them plenty of opportunities for flirtatious behavior.

In many ways, this pair fulfills each other's needs. If they can iron out their few differences and learn to communicate with one another on a deeper level, they may eventually form a lasting union.

Sagittarius with Cancer

(June 22–July 23)

T hough these signs have very different points of view, the Archer and the Crab can supply the missing ingredients in each other's lives.

Sagittarius is a fire sign, who loves travel, adventure, and freedom. Cancer is a nurturing water sign, who needs home, family, and security. In an ideal situation, Cancer would create a home base for Sagittarius, while giving the independent Archer a large degree of freedom. In turn, the Archer would introduce the Crab to a much broader range of experiences.

To Cancer, family will always be the first priority. This sign reveres all family traditions and enjoys visits to Mother and other favorite relatives. Sagittarius, however, left home early and never looked back. Though the Archer may give unselfishly to loved ones and feel a strong affection for its family, the bonds of childhood are long past.

Communication between this pair requires refinements on both sides. Sagittarius's naturally blunt, direct style may easily wound the sensitive Crab. And though the Archer may initially be fascinated by the Crab's mysterious ways, it may soon tire of Cancer's touchy moods, which it can't understand. Cancer must attempt to speak its mind—even when it hurts.

Money is another sensitive area for this pair. Cancer wants and needs security—the kind that comes from money in the bank. Sagittarius is a gambler and a spendthrift who spreads money around like fertilizer—to nourish its dreams.

It is when the chips are down that these two will most appreciate each other. Cancer's nurturing helps revive the Archer when it's feeling down-and-out; Sagittarius's sunny optimism will be a boon to the Crab when pessimism clouds its outlook. This pair can get each other back on their feet in no time.

A desire to please and plenty of patience will be necessary to make this combination sizzle in the bedroom. Sagittarius will have to intuit what will please the sensual, but nonverbal, Cancer. And Cancer will have to learn to appreciate the Archer's playful approach to lovemaking.

Compromise may be tricky for these two. However, A loving home and adventurous life awaits them if they are successful.

Sagittarius with Leo
(July 24–August 23)

Relationships with Leo are always easy provided you acknowledge one thing: Leo rules. Can the independent Archer, who would never subject itself to a ruler, hook up happily with this bossy sign?

The outlook is not as bleak as one might suppose. A natural sympathy exists between Leo and Sagittarius because they have so many traits in common.

Both of them are optimistic, generous, and dramatic fire signs who believe anything is possible. They are lavish spenders with similar ideas about money and lifestyle. Both are endowed with social graces and are always welcome and popular guests at any gathering.

It's in their personal styles that conflicts arise. The Lion is a born commander; the Archer is a born rebel. Sagittarius will do anything for someone it cares about—except take orders. Nothing will send the Archer packing faster than being told what to do. Leo had better check its domineering ways at the door—or risk finding the house empty.

Sagittarius must tread lightly around

49

the Lion's ego. Leo appreciates the Archer's honesty and humor—but only when it is directed at others. The unvarnished truth about itself is not for the Lion; gloss it over with a compliment or two and strife can be avoided.

Both of these signs are hot-tempered and numerous small eruptions are likely to occur when they get together. Each is quick to forgive and forget, but Sagittarius, and not the proud Lion, will always have to be the first to apologize.

These two are dreamers: Sagittarius's dreams are many and varied; Leo's are few and constant. But any temptation to create a business partnership to realize one of their dreams should be resisted. Vision they have; practicality they lack.

Lovemaking for these two should be delightful and uninhibited, ranging from playful to passionate. Of course, the blunt Archer shouldn't talk too much in the bedroom—the less said, the less chance of offense.

If Sagittarius and Leo can avoid becoming locked in a power struggle, they should be able to forge a lasting and exciting relationship.

Sagittarius with Virgo

(August 24–September 23)

T hese two signs approach just about everything from opposite directions. The question is, will they meet in the middle?

The Archer starts big and scales down; the Virgin starts small and builds up. The Archer has a grand plan for a house—then pares it down to fit practical and financial restrictions. The Virgin has a house plan, too, which it builds up detail by detail with one eye on the budget and the other on the clock. Virgo focuses on the details and points out weak spots in the Archer's grand schemes—not a habit Sagittarius will welcome. But from Virgo's down-to-earth point of view, the fiery Sagittarian expansiveness seems impractical, even foolhardy.

Talk for these two is usually easy; understanding is often difficult. And since they look at life through opposite ends of a telescope, this couple may never connect unless they make a strong effort to explain themselves to each other. Arguments won't last long with these two since both are flexible signs.

However, this flexibility can work against them if, rather than striving to understand each other, one or the other just gives in—sacrificing important needs and fostering resentment. Real understanding can lead to compromises that won't violate either sign's unique individuality.

These two have much to offer each other as business or marriage partners. The Virgin provides stability without the stuffiness that usually bores the Archer. The rebellious Archer takes direction and guidance easily from the practical Virgo, who can teach this sign to use its wild energy in constructive ways. Virgo will admire Sagittarius's

54

dreams, but will also demand results—and will prod Sagittarius until it produces some. In return, Sagittarius can help Virgo broaden its horizons and seek larger goals in life.

Sexually, Sagittarius's sense of fun helps the more serious Virgo overcome inhibitions, while Virgo pampers the Archer with tender, loving care.

Though this relationship is challenging, it can be a powerful combination, especially if both signs make the effort to understand their partner's differences while staying true to themselves.

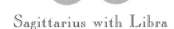

Sagittarius with Libra

(September 24–October 23)

L ibra suits Sagittarius so well that the Archer may need a pinch— just to be sure it's not dreaming.

At first, Sagittarius will be flattered by the way Libra makes this sign feel like a font of wisdom. A skilled listener, Libra will never directly challenge the Archer. Instead the sign of the Scales presents any opposing points of view simply as logical options, which the Archer can easily accept.

A cool air sign, Libra is warmed by Sagittarius's fiery enthusiasm. Since the Scales are forever weighing pros and cons, they often miss out on a full range of physical and emotional experiences. The Archer introduces Libra to an exciting new world of risk and adventure.

As the marriage sign of the zodiac, Libra will want a commitment but will wait patiently for freedom-loving Sagittarius to come around. And while it is waiting, the Scales could be the perfect traveling companion for the wandering Archer.

This pair has much going for them as lovers, friends, or business partners. Temperamentally, they are both outgoing optimists. Libra rarely competes or tries to be boss, like some other signs. Both enjoy socializing with all kinds of people, and a gracious, diplomatic Libra, who can make small talk better than any other sign, can be quite a social asset to an upward-aspiring Archer.

Neither partner suffers from jealousy—a big plus. Both enjoy harmless flirtations and won't feel threatened by the other's roving eye. Because each sign has a high moral code and values honesty above all else, they are likely to trust each other. However, Libra may feel left out, if restless Sagittarius decides to take off on a solitary adventure. Chances are, however, that the

Archer will soon miss Libra's charming companionship.

Emotional and hot-tempered, the Archer almost never hesitates to express its feelings. Libra's more cool and distant behavior can be unsettling for the spontaneous Archer—though the discomfort will cause only minor problems in this relationship.

Sexually, this mix of fire and air signs works like a fan on each other's desires. Love opens new worlds to Sagittarius, which it will be happy to explore with Libra for a long time.

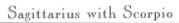

Sagittarius with Scorpio

(October 24–November 22)

C an a Sagittarius, who lays all its cards on the table, get together with a Scorpio, who plays its cards close to the chest? Scorpio says only what is necessary; Sagittarius says way too much. This is an unlikely pairing—but not impossible.

An intense water sign, Scorpio admires the honest, straight-talking Sagittarius. Life is much sunnier for Scorpio when it is warmed with the fiery Archer's optimism. And this cagey sign is more likely to take a few risks when inspired by Sagittarius. In turn, the Archer's arrows head straight to their mark under the strong, stable influence of the Scorpion.

Appreciation of these positive qualities can help this couple overcome some significant differences. Most important is Scorpio's need for control versus Sagittarius's need for independence. This difference can lead to an on-again–off-again relationship with these two. And Scorpio's emotional reticence can be baffling to the open and forthcoming Archer. Sagittarius must learn to tread carefully with Scorpio, who does not take life casually and will not laugh off the Archer's tactless or thoughtless behavior. Scorpio doesn't get angry—it gets even. However, because Scorpio can detect that Sagittarius's motives are not premeditated or threatening, the legendary sting of the Scorpion may not be necessary.

It may take time for these signs to trust each other, but when they do, their relationship will smooth out. Eventually, Scorpio will understand that the free-roaming Sagittarius is not up to mischief. However, to keep Scorpio happy, Sagittarius should avoid disappearing each time a new adventure beckons.

Scorpio offers Sagittarius a stable

foundation and a chance for accomplishment. When the Archer wants to achieve a goal, Scorpio's loyalty and unwavering moral support will prove invaluable.

This is a highly combustible combination sexually, especially when Sagittarius's athletic prowess meshes with Scorpio's sustained passion.

Though Sagittarius may have to give up some freedom and Scorpio may have to give up some control, the results should make these adjustments worthwhile.

Sagittarius with Sagittarius

(November 23–December 21)

These two members of the most freedom-loving sign of the zodiac could make perfect traveling companions down the road of life.

Who better than another Archer to understand the burning need to follow one's own quest in life? Each knows why the other partner feels the urge to fight city hall or run with the wind. And neither will hold the other back.

Whenever two people of the same sign meet, there is always a sympathetic attraction. The basic openness of this couple keeps everything aboveboard. However, a relationship between two spontaneous fire signs might become combative. The slightest provocation may cause tempers to flare—but as usual with these signs, fights will be over quickly and soon forgotten.

Once committed to each other, this pair will have no trouble agreeing on important issues, such as where to live or whether to have children. Home life is likely to be a bit chaotic with a jolly jumble of pets, children, and projects. Neither sign likes to adhere to a schedule or limit others with rules and restrictions.

Two Sagittarians will share the same desires: to know more, see everything, and be where the action is. They're never bored and are constantly introducing each other to something new.

For a lasting relationship, this pair must have shared goals and interests. Strong political ideals, similar careers, or common spiritual pursuits could bond this couple together. If these two break up, they usually remain on good terms, since they are too much alike not to respect each other.

Sexually, these fire signs should communicate beautifully and provide each other with enough variety to sustain their initial passion. However, if they do not share outside interests, they may head off in different directions. And, if Sagittarius is not near the one it loves, this sign tends to love the one it's near.

Two Archers must rely on more than luck and the spontaneous passion of soul mates to hold them together. Taking aim at the same targets is one way to ensure that these two remain together for the great adventure of life.

Sagittarius with Capricorn

(December 22–January 20)

W hy is footloose Sagittarius attracted to disciplined, ambitious Capricorn? Perhaps because the sign of the Goat can help the Archer hit its mark.

Steady, materialistic, and earthy, Capricorn can lead the Archer up the path to achievement. The Goat is a great teacher of self-discipline, which the Archer needs in order to make its dreams come true.

In return, Sagittarius performs a valuable service for Capricorn: It shows the Goat that there is more to life than work. Sagittarius can get the Goat to kick up its heels, try new things, and explore new ideas. They'll complement each other in business or stimulate each other as friends.

These signs boost each other's self-confidence. The Goat's worries about the future lessen under the umbrella of Sagittarius's optimism. And when conservative Capricorn teaches the Archer how to save money and pay attention to details, it frees the Archer to do what it likes best—explore new territory.

The Goat will be charmed by Sagittarius's humor and lighthearted sense of fun. The Archer might even inspire Capricorn to throw caution to the wind and enjoy life to the fullest, especially in the bedroom.

There is much for these signs to admire in each other, such as the courageous way Sagittarius speaks the truth. The thick-skinned Goat won't be put off by the Archer's bluntness or lack of tact. Sagittarius will admire the way Capricorn assumes responsibility. If the Goat sets up a loose structure for running the household, the Archer might be tempted to settle down. Capricorn must remember, however, to give Sagittarius plenty of slack—or risk defection.

The biggest hurdle for this couple is financial. Sagittarius will want to spend money enjoying life or helping others, while Capricorn will want to buy things—a house or car. The best way to resolve this conflict is discuss common goals together and work out a compromise.

Once these two learn what each other wants from life, they may find that they can complement each other in pursuit of their goals. Their differences may be complementary as well—and life together be good.

Sagittarius with Aquarius

(January 21–February 19)

This pair is fundamentally in agreement; morally and intellectually they are on the same wavelength, yet they fight like a pair of rough-and-tumble puppies. They may look like they're trying to kill each other but they're enjoying themselves immensely.

Like Sagittarius, Aquarius loves reaching out to others. However, the

Water Bearer often feels like an oddball who doesn't quite blend in. This sign's eccentric point of view, which often sets it apart, endears the Water Bearer to the adventurous Sagittarius.

Emotionally, the fiery Sagittarius heats up the cool, airy Aquarius—just what the Water Bearer needs. And there is powerful sexual chemistry between the Water Bearer and the Archer when they share erotic adventures.

Basic friendship between this pair also runs deep. They understand and appreciate one another's approach to life. Both think expansively, aiming to make the world a better place. Sagittarius wants freedom for everyone, while

Aquarius wants equality—two positive goals that are different enough to spark spirited discussions. Both have strong political opinions though Aquarius is the one more likely to act on them.

When this pair turns to personal issues, they'll have equally spirited exchanges. Aquarius won't flinch under the brutal honesty of Sagittarius. In fact, this sign is capable of dispensing the hard truth in return—and the Archer had better be able to take it.

In a committed relationship, Sagittarius may bump up against Aquarius's deep need for privacy. Though the Water Bearer may preach revolution for the world, it won't appreciate any similar intrusion in its personal life.

Each sign supports and strengthens the other's individuality. Sagittarius makes Aquarius laugh and the Water Bearer makes Sagittarius focus—both difficult tasks. At the same time, both signs feel at ease with each other. Neither is going to tie the other down or interfere with the other's outside interests.

If both stand their ground, Sagittarius and Aquarius can have a lifetime of serious fun, stimulating arguments, and rousing adventures.

Sagittarius with Pisces

(February 20–March 20)

Both of these signs are explorers: Sagittarius probes the outer, physical landscape and Pisces explores the inner, emotional landscape.

Both are flexible, mutable signs that thrive on freedom and chafe under rules and responsibilities. These that are kindred souls moving in different territories.

The Archer is fascinated by the mysterious Fish, while Pisces admires the outgoing Archer, a sign that is able to share its passions with the outside world. This fascinates the introverted Fish, who responds to the world intuitively but lacks the ability to interact physically with the same positive energy.

Both must understand and accept each other's differences before they can meet on common ground. Sagittarius believes that truth is simple, unchangeable, black or white. Pisces lives in a world of gray, where truth is shaded by each person's individual emotional reality. Sagittarius deals with the facts of the matter; Pisces deals with the feelings.

As a water sign, Pisces is always con-

scious of what might hurt someone. Sagittarius puts the plain truth ahead of any other considerations, which is bound to complicate matters with this couple. When the Archer's blunt honesty hurts Pisces' sensitive feelings, Sagittarius can become exasperated and impatient.

The Archer must learn to express opinions in a nonthreatening way if this sign wishes to get along with the sensitive Fish. Arguing, one of Sagittarius's talents, loses points with Pisces, who tends to talk around issues, rather than confront them directly. When Sagittarius demands a straight answer or an emotional truth from Pisces, the Fish gets defensive—believing the Archer should just instinctively know what and how it feels. It is Pisces' challenge to learn to express its feelings in a way the Archer can understand.

Sexually, however, these two bring out each other's creative, playful side. Sagittarius's fiery passion blazes hotter when fueled by Pisces' imagination. This is not an easy pairing, but one full of possibilities. For it to work, Sagittarius must become more considerate of Pisces' feelings and the Fish must provide the Archer with the keys to its inner kingdom.

The text of this book was set in Bembo
and the display in Caslon Open Face
by Crane Typesetting Service, Inc.,
West Barnstable, Massachusetts.

Book design and illustrations by
JUDITH A. STAGNITTO